DE-FENSE!

Doug Marx

The Rourke Corporation, Inc.
Vero Beach, Florida 32964

The Rourke Corporation, Inc.
P.O. Box 3328, Vero Beach, FL 32964

Marx, Doug.
    De-fense!/by Doug Marx.
        p. cm. — (Football heroes)
    Includes bibliographical references (p. 47) and index.
    Summary. Discusses defense strategies in football, such positions as linebacker and cornerback, and various notable defense players in the history of the sport.
    ISBN 0-86593-152-6
    1. Football—United States—Defense—Juvenile literature.
2. Football players—United States—Biography—Juvenile literature.
{1. Football—Defense.} I. Title. II. Title: Defense.
III. Series.
GV951.18.M86 1992
796.332'2—dc20   92-8763
                                                                     CIP
                                                                      AC

Series Editor: Gregory Lee
Editor: Marguerite Aronowitz
Book design and production: The Creative Spark, San Clemente, CA
Cover photograph: Jim Commentucci/ALLSPORT

Contents

Charles Haley is bad news for offensive linemen and quarterbacks. He is one of the leading pass rushers in the NFC.

Unsung Heroes

The date: January 28, 1990. The site: the Louisiana Superdome in New Orleans. The event: Super Bowl XXIV, a game many think of as the greatest championship football game ever played—by one team. Playing to perfection, the San Francisco 49ers, led by quarterback Joe Montana, crushed the Denver Broncos. The final score: 49ers 55, Broncos 10.

The 49ers went on a rampage, setting 18 Super Bowl records along the way, including most points in one game and widest margin of victory. Looking back, what fans remember most about the lopsided victory was Montana's pinpoint passing and the explosive 49er offense. Perhaps what fans ought to remember was a 49er defense that sacked Denver quarterback John Elway four times, intercepted him twice, forced four turnovers, and manhandled the Bronco offense.

Everyone remembers the names of the 49er's offensive stars in that game: Montana, his pass-catching partner Jerry Rice, and running back Roger Craig. But who can name the defensive heroes? For example, tackles Michael Carter and Pierce Holt, who contained the Broncos' ground attack. Or big-play man and linebacker Charles Haley, who led the sack attack. Or Ronnie Lott, one of the game's all-time outstanding safeties and an eight-time Pro Bowler who locked up the Bronco secondary.

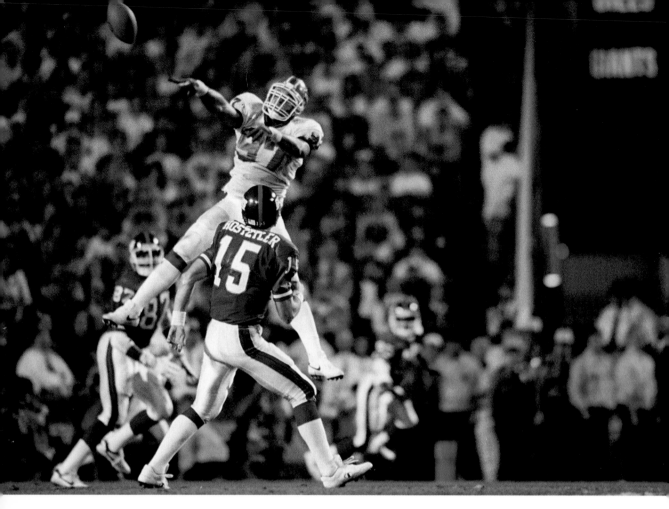

Every fan watches the team with the football, but watching a great defense in action is exciting, too. That's Cornelius Bennett getting airborne during Super Bowl XXV.

Defense

The critical play of Super Bowl XXIV may have come midway through the first quarter, when the Broncos still looked as if they had a chance. With the score only 7-3 in favor of the 49ers, the Broncos had a first down at mid-field and were determined to get their game going. Elway handed off to running back Bobby Humphrey, slicing off-tackle. Humphrey ran right into the arms of 49er tight end Kevin Fagan, who tore the ball right out of his hands. 49er safety Chet Brooks recovered the fumble and the Broncos' fate was sealed. Their momentum lost and their spirit broken, the Broncos' game went from bad to worse.

Defense. Or, as the word is sometimes chanted by stadium crowds, "DE-FENSE! DE-FENSE! DE-FENSE!" Defense is the other half of the game, the other side of football. It's the world of huge, 300-pound linemen bearing down on a quarterback for the sack. It is the helmet-to-helmet, head-on collision at the scrimmage line between a fullback and a middle linebacker, like elk locking horns. It is the world of the blitz, of the blocked kick and fumble, of the interception returned for a touchdown. It is the spectacular hit, when an end leaps high to catch a pass and has his legs knocked out from under him. And it is the heart-stopping, goal-line stand—one of the most dramatic moments in football.

Defense. It is the world of unsung heroes. The number of defensive stars who have made it to the Football Hall of Fame can be counted on your fingers and toes. In this book we will name some of these players and give them their due glory. We will look at the skills, positions, basic fundamentals, and strategies that make defensive football every bit as exciting as offensive football. Along the way, we will discuss the fact that defense is—above all—a team game.

History

Football is one of our oldest sports. Versions of soccer and rugby—the earliest forms of football—were played in ancient China and in the days of the Roman Empire. In the early 1600s, American settlers would choose up sides and kick an air-filled animal bladder around the village streets.

In the 1800s, the game became popular among college students. Young men would get together and play a rough-and-tumble version of "football" that was nothing like the game we know today. It fast became a favorite sport on college campuses.

These contests were all brawn and no brains, however, with 15 to 25 players on a side. Dogpiles and gang tackles were common. Fullbacks with lots of blockers would smash right up the middle into a defensive wall.

Then a man named Walter Camp, known as the "Father of American Football," invented some new rules that created the scrimmage line, the center snap, and the role of quarterback. The team was fixed at eleven players. Other features of the new game included downs and the kickoff. Still, even with these changes, football remained a violent sport that lacked grace and beauty. In 1905 alone there were 18 deaths and 159 life-threatening injuries recorded in American college play!

The Passing Game

In 1906 the forward pass was legalized in an attempt to make the game safer and more interesting. The changes worked, and suddenly football became a little less brutal and a little more strategic. Before the pass was introduced, the problems of defense were simple: stop the runner at all costs. The punishment was awful. Wearing little in the way of protection—leather helmets without face masks and thin shoulder pads—seven linemen either stood up or crouched at the scrimmage line. They used their fists to get at the runner. As the game became modernized, coaching and game strategy became more important.

As the passing game evolved, the old nine- and seven-man defensive lines were reduced to a six-man line to create better coverage. By the 1930s yet another lineman was dropped back, leaving a five-man front wall. Through the post-World War II years of pro football, the front line shrunk again and again. A four- or three-man line is used today.

As the game itself became more sophisticated, so

did the equipment. Players now are outfitted like Roman gladiators. Helmets, face masks and mouthpieces, along with hip, thigh, shoulder, knee, shin, and rib pads, are a player's tools of the trade.

Along with these improvements came the better defensive players. Recently, defensive players have become stars in their own right. Defenders such as "Mean" Joe Green and William "Refrigerator" Perry became household names during the 1970s and '80s, finally receiving the ultimate modern tribute—they can be seen on television commercials!

Despite the individual attention some defensive players have received, however, defensive football remains a team game. For many years, defensive statistics—plays such as fumble recoveries and sacks—were only recorded as team efforts. It has just been in the last 15 years or so that individual records have been kept for sacks, tackles, and forced fumbles.

Great defensive teams are better remembered than individual players. The Miami Dolphins' "No-Name" defense of the early 1970s, the great "Steel Curtain" defense of the Steelers through the late '70s, and the "Stinging Bee" defense of the 49ers that dominated the 1980s are three examples.

As the years have gone by and the game has changed, defensive football has gone from methods of sheer brute strength to speed, complexity, and technique. Defense is now a part of a coordinated game plan, and each player has an assignment that must be carried out correctly if the plan is to work.

*One of the best defensive ends is Charles Mann, who is great against
the run and often forces quarterbacks to hurry and throw.*

Defensive Strategies

Defensive formations are the most complicated of any in football. Gone are the days of the brawny, slow-footed, seven-man line set up like a wall of muscle against the offense. In fact, in the course of today's game it is unlikely that a defense will ever set up in the same formation twice in a row. Depending on the offensive lineup, the defensive unit might counter with a 4-3, a 3-4, a flex, a dog, a blitz, a zone, or a man-to-man strategy. As if these formations are not confusing enough, there are variations called stacks, slants, stunts, and pinches, together with new trends such as the dime and nickel multiple back defenses. To make things even more complicated, a defensive team may shift from one to the other right up to the moment the ball is snapped.

Defense Trivia

Q: Name the only player to make three interceptions in one Super Bowl game.

A: Rod Martin of the Oakland Raiders stole three passes from the Philadelphia Eagles in Super Bowl XV (1980). He did not receive the game MVP, however. That honor went to Raiders quarterback Jim Plunkett.

Q: Who is the all-time leader in interceptions?

A: Paul Krause, who stole 81 passes in 16 seasons for a total of 1,185 yards and three touchdowns.

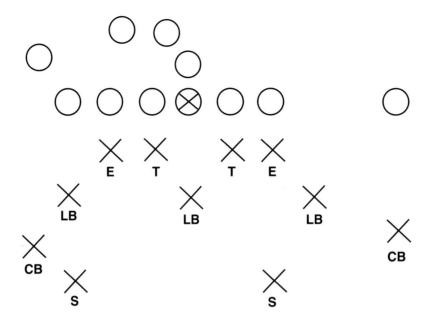

The 4-3 defense puts two tackles and two ends on the scrimmage line, backed up by three linebackers.

To understand how specialized the defensive game has become, it is helpful to take a look at modern strategy.

4-3 Defense

Throughout the 1950s, '60s, and '70s, the most common defensive lineup in pro football was the *4-3*. This means a front line of four defenders, with three linebackers backing them up. This formation provides a defense that can handle a balanced run-pass attack (that is, 60 percent running, 40 percent passing). At the line of scrimmage two defensive tackles line up opposite the offensive guards. Two defensive ends flank these tackles, playing just to the outside of the offensive tackles.

The middle linebacker, who plays slightly in back of and between the two defensive tackles, is the key to the 4-3 defense. He has the clearest view of the opposing team. In a sense, he is the defensive quarterback. The

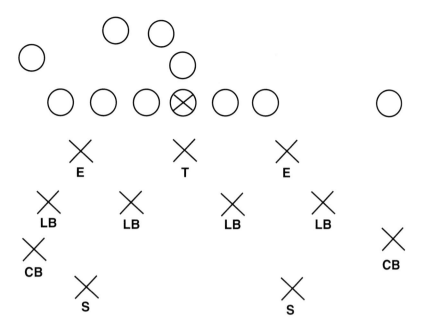

The 3-4 defense uses a nose tackle and two defensive ends only, keeping four linebackers at large for better coverage.

outside linebackers must be flexible and ready to defend against a pass or a run. These three linebackers never set up exactly the same way. They are always shifting around behind the defensive linemen, both to confuse the opponent's offense and to get in better position for the play they think is coming.

Although the 3-4 defense became popular in the 1980s and '90s, the 4-3 is still used a great deal. In both of these formations, two cornerbacks and two safeties are set in the *secondary*, the defensive backfield.

3-4 Defense

Currently the most popular defense in pro football, the *3-4* defense is made up of a nose tackle flanked by two ends on the scrimmage line, and supported by four linebackers. The nose tackle is the key to the 3-4 defense. Lining up across from the center, he must be strong enough to control the two offensive guards as well—three on one! To succeed, a nose tackle must be quick, strong, and agile.

In the 3-4, the four linebackers have more flexibility than their counterparts in the 4-3. The two middle (or inside) linebackers roam the area behind the three linemen, ready to cut off the run. The two outside linebackers must also try to contain the run, and all four must be fast enough to handle their pass coverage duties. Again, these four linebackers are never fixed in position. Depending on the offensive play, they can rush, stay where they are, or drop back for better pass coverage. As with the 4-3 defense, these defenders are shifting all the time, trying to upset the offense and confuse blockers as to where the rush is coming from.

The most important advantage of the 3-4 is that it puts one more player in the backfield for pass coverage.

The Flex

The *flex* defense is a variation on the 4-3. It is designed to stop the run and is, therefore, somewhat weak as a pass defense. The flex puts seven men near the line of scrimmage. Two stay on the line, two drop back a couple of steps, and the linebackers group around behind. There is no rule as to which of the four linemen hold the line or drop back. This creates a staggered front line, rather than a four-man wall. The linemen who drop back slightly do not rush the quarterback. They wait to see what happens before making their move. They must read the play, then react to the ball.

Other Defenses

Stacks, slants, stunts, and pinches are tactics and positions taken up by individual linemen and linebackers to confuse the offense and discover holes in the offensive line.

In a *stack*, one or more of the linebackers "stacks

An intimidating defense is often led by a strong player, such as veteran Ronnie Lott.

up" directly behind a defensive lineman, making it impossible for the offense to know which way he is going to move.

In a *slant*, a defensive lineman charges to the left or right of his offensive opponent, rather than head-on. This makes it difficult for the blocker to know how to position himself.

The *stunt* is a tricky play where one defender (lineman or linebacker) loops or circles around a teammate, switching their rushing paths. This action only happens once the ball is snapped. The objective is to confuse the offense and to create gaps in the offensive line that might be more easily penetrated by a fellow defensive teammate.

One of the NFL's best defensive tackles was Merlin Olsen (right), a member of the Rams' legendary 4-3 defense, the "Fearsome Foursome."

In *pinch* plays, the defensive linemen set up in the gaps between the offensive linemen. Rather than take on the offensive linemen one-on-one, they double-team or "pinch" them. This usually gets one offensive blocker completely out of the way, creating enough room for a linebacker to rush through and sack the quarterback.

Dogs and *blitzes* put extreme pressure on the passing game. A dog is a surprise pass rush by one or more linebackers. A blitz brings the cornerbacks and safeties rushing in as well. The dog can sometimes be used to defend against a run, but a blitz is designed to only stop a pass. Timing is important in these strategies, because if the quarterback can see a dog or blitz coming, he will take advantage of the situation, often for a long gain.

Man-To-Man and Zone Defenses

The *man-to-man* pass defense was commonly used in the 1950s and '60s. It calls for a one-on-one situation in which one defender covers one pass receiver. Linebackers pick up running backs on pass patterns, and cornerbacks and safeties pick up the ends. As the passing game has improved, the man-to-man has become a risky defense, giving way to the zone.

In the 1970s and '80s the *zone* became the principal defense against the pass. In the zone, defenders cover an area or zone, rather than an individual receiver. Instead of picking up a receiver as he runs through his pattern, zone defenders hold their ground, reacting once the ball is thrown. With the ball in the air, defenders then converge on their target. The zone is intended to reduce the chances of a breakaway play for a long gain or touchdown.

New Trends

As the passing game has become more sophisticated, defending against it has likewise changed. Recent defensive strategy involves adding one, two, or three extra defenders to the secondary. The 4-3 and 3-4 setups leave four players to handle coverage. When a fifth defender is added, the team is using the *nickel* defense. A sixth defender creates a *dime* defense. These extra pass defenders allow a team to double- and triple-team individual receivers. In today's play, strong passing teams often send as many as five receivers downfield, which makes the use of "multiple defensive backs" a must.

Defensive tackle and Pro Bowler Keith Millard earns his money the hard way.

Linemen And Linebackers

I n football, each play starts from the scrimmage line. It is the first point of contact. First the offense and defense face off, the quarterback shouts "23, red, 42, green, hut-hut-hut," and then BAM! The linemen collide head-on with a fury that makes the ground shake. Plays are made or broken in that moment of thunder that follows the lightning snap of the ball. It is where defense begins.

Tackles

In today's popular 3-4 defense the middle lineman, or nose tackle, is expected to control fully half of the offensive line. It is his job to take on the center and two offensive guards, and to stop or prevent any run up the middle.

In recent years the Minnesota Vikings' Keith Millard stands out among the finest of defensive tackles. Millard has all the skills a great lineman needs. He can explode out of his three-point stance the instant the ball is snapped and be moving full speed in just three or four steps. At six-feet, five-inches, he has exceptional balance and can change direction instantly. And he is strong enough to battle as many as three blockers while reacting to a ball carrier.

During the 1989 season, Millard was named the Associated Press Player of the Year. He racked up an amazing 12 tackles and two sacks in one four-game stretch. A one-man wall when it comes to stopping the run, Millard is also a relentless pass rusher. His 18 sacks in 1989 tied a league record for sacks by a tackle. As a team, the Vikings were number one in overall defense in the 1988 and 1989 seasons. With Millard out with a serious knee injury, the Vikings dropped to number 13 in 1990, having a 6-10 won-lost record. This shows how crucial a defensive tackle can be to a team.

Millard could be Hall of Fame bound, an honor given only to eight defensive tackles in the history of the game. Hall of Famers of yesteryear include Leo "The Lion" Nomellini and "Mean" Joe Greene.

Other young tackles to watch and learn from during the 1990s include Michael Dean Perry of the Cleveland Browns and the Detroit Lions' Jerry Ball. The 49ers' Michael Carter almost defined the position through San Francisco's glory years.

Ends

What makes the sack statistics of a tackle like Keith Millard so impressive is that it is usually the other linemen—the defensive ends—who make that big play. Positioned outside of (or flanking) the tackles, the ends can charge the quarterback while the tackles put pressure on the offensive line.

Defensive ends are like three players in one. They must be strong enough to take on inside runs, quick enough to handle any run or run-pass options that come wide to their side, and still act as the primary pass rushers. This means they must be quick as a linebacker and strong as a tackle. And they have to wait just long enough to judge how the play is going to break, then react.

Unlike tackles, whose focus is the middle of the

Reggie White is known to his teammates as "The Minister of Defense," and his ministry includes the most sacks of any other player since he entered the NFL in 1985.

offensive line, ends play the situation. They play closer in or farther out, depending on whether a run or pass is expected. The defensive end focuses on the running back nearest to him, the offensive tackle, and the quarterback.

There are some great Hall of Fame ends, among them Carl Eller and Deacon Jones. Today's crop of defensive ends, or "sack masters," are rewriting the record books. The Philadelphia Eagles' Reggie White is a standout and future Hall of Famer. Since coming to the NFL in 1985, White has led the pack with an astounding 96 sacks—more than any other player. White is so good he is often double- and triple-teamed, but not even this pressure can stop him. White has class, ability, and respect. He is one of the most revered and feared players in pro football.

Buffalo Bills' Bruce "I Am the Greatest" Smith was the NFL's Defensive Player of the Year in 1990, with 19 sacks. Smith finished that season with an incredible 99 tackles—and 82 of them were unassisted! Known as the master of the "rip and spin," Smith combines brute strength and tremendous speed to fight off his offensive opponents and terrorize the quarterback.

Some defensive ends weigh nearly 300 pounds, giving them unbelievable explosive power. Chris Doleman, teammate of Viking tackle Keith Millard, also has Hall of Fame potential. In 1990, thanks to Millard's strength jamming up the middle, Doleman recorded a team-high 21 sacks.

Last but not least, veteran Richard Dent of the Chicago Bears turned in an amazing three interceptions during the 1990 season. The big-play man for the Bears' defense with excellent speed and agility, Dent makes the life of offensive tackles miserable. He was named MVP in the Bears' 1985 Super Bowl rout of the New England Patriots (46-10). Dent forced two fumbles and put so much pressure on the Pats' offense that it was a miracle they scored at all. During the regular 1985 season he led the NFL in sacks, tipped two passes that were intercepted and run back for touchdowns, forced another interception that went for a TD, and scored on an interception himself! Not a bad "offensive" display for a season's defensive work.

Linebackers

In the early decades of pro football, the position of linebacker did not exist. With a six-man front line, the closest thing to a linebacker was a defensive center. When most teams went to a five-man line in the 1940s, the back-up defenders became known as linebackers,

You can run but you can't hide from the Bears' Mike Singletary, the best middle linebacker of the 1980s.

Dick Butkus (51) was the Bears' answer to the running games of the 1970s. This linebacker is now in the NFL Hall of Fame.

but the position was not given All-Pro team recognition until 1952.

One of the most famous linebackers of all time is Hall of Famer Sam Huff, who held down the middle for the Giants in the 1950s and 1960s. When a documentary was being made about him, the film crew wired a microphone inside his helmet. For the first time, fans were treated to an inside look at the defensive game. In the movie Huff defined the tough, ornery, hard-hitting reputation of linebackers. Since then, and especially during the 1970s, linebackers have become indispensable to the modern defensive game. Other great Hall of Fame names of yesteryear are the Green Bay Packers' Ray Nitschke, the Bears' Dick Butkus, and Jack Lambert of the Pittsburgh Steelers.

Butkus once observed that "desire," a "competitive mean streak," and "football instinct" are the essential qualities of a good linebacker. Linebackers, weighing in at around 220 pounds, must be strong, fast, and smart. Besides shutting down the running game, they must also be dangerous pass rushers and capable of making interceptions. This calls for good ball chasing ability.

Physical skills are not enough for greatness, however. The middle or inside linebacker is the "quarterback" of the defensive team. He must be a leader. Eye-to-eye with the quarterback, he commands the best view of the offense. He must be able to read the offensive play the moment the ball is snapped, make the tackles on all running plays, or help out the deep backs on passes. It is the basic job of the outside, or corner linebackers, to force a ball carrier into the middle where he can be tackled.

The best middle linebacker of the 1980s was the Bears' Mike Singletary. An even six-feet tall and 228 pounds, the veteran Singletary has been the heart and soul of the Bears' defense. An eight-time Pro Bowler and two-time NFL Defensive Player of the Year, he once set a personal record of 20 tackles in an overtime game against the Denver Broncos! A born leader known for his spirit and intensity, Singletary is considered a class player with a possible future as an NFL head coach.

With the 4-3 defense giving way to the 3-4, the roaming middle linebackers are giving way to inside linebackers. Coming off a fantastic 1990 Super Bowl season, Thomas "Pepper" Johnson of the Giants will no doubt tear up the league in years to come. Another inside linebacker, John Offerdahl, is also destined for

*"L.T."—Lawrence Taylor—is the fans' unanimous choice for a
Hall of Fame linebacker.*

the Hall of Fame. Racking up more than 100 tackles in three of his five Pro Bowl seasons, Offerdahl was twice the Miami Dolphins' nominee for the NFL Man of the Year award, which reflects his leadership abilities.

When it comes to outside linebackers, none can compare with the Giants' Lawrence Taylor, who dominated the 1980s. Taylor is, simply, the greatest outside linebacker in NFL history. Playing his position with freedom, abandon, and brilliance, Taylor has made it to the Pro Bowl a record-breaking ten times, leading everyone with a career 124.5 sacks. A sure bet for Hall of Fame honors, Taylor was unanimously elected to the NFL's 1980s "Team of the Decade."

Derrick Thomas of the Kansas City Chiefs may be the linebacker of the future. In only his second year of pro play, Thomas led the NFL with 20 sacks in 1990. Seven of those sacks came in one game against the Seattle Seahawks! Those who saw the game rate Thomas' performance as one of the all-time wonders of individual defensive play. He is so fast—40 yards in 4.52 seconds—that offensive tackles do not have a chance against him.

The only player who might have a chance of matching Thomas is Pat Swilley of the New Orleans Saints. Averaging 10 sacks per season in his first five years as a pro, Swilley has emerged as a premier outside linebacker who still has many prime years ahead of him.

One of the fastest men in the NFL is cornerback Ron Woodson.

Cornerbacks And Safeties

Imagine for a moment the following game situation: The Rams have the ball on their own 30-yard line. It is third and ten. Wide receiver Henry Ellard moves out to the left and the Steelers' Rod Woodson, maybe the best cornerback in the game today, comes up to meet him man-to-man.

The ball is snapped. Woodson bumps Ellard at the scrimmage line, trying to upset his timing and pattern. Then the two players streak down the sideline, step for step, like race horses heading for a photo finish. Rams' quarterback Jim Everett goes deep in the pocket, looking long for a touchdown, and fires a bull's eye downfield. It is a perfect pass, but at the last second—just as Ellard seems sure of catching the ball—Woodson leaps like a dancer and tips the ball away without touching his man. Incomplete pass.

Fourth and ten. The Rams have to punt. Who drops back for the kick? Woodson. Settling under a high spiral, he makes the catch and sprints zig-zag up the middle, picking up blockers, dodging tacklers, and crossing the goal line a few seconds later for the six points. That is the kind of day a great cornerback can have. Preventing a touchdown one minute, scoring one the next!

Cornerbacks

Cornerbacks and safeties are the last line of defense. This is the place where risk and daring come into the game: the littlest mistake can often cost six points. Although they are no slouches when it comes to the hard hit, cornerbacks give the defensive game its agility and grace, thrills and spills. On top of strength, brains, and quickness, cornerbacks require sure hands and the kind of speed that covers 100 yards in 10-plus seconds. Sometimes they must do it all while running backward! No wonder the best cornerbacks also return punts and kickoffs.

Whether the setup is a zone or a man-to-man, the cornerback is matched up with a wide receiver. It is a slippery job, made up of the fastest men in football. A cornerback should cover his opponent so well that a quarterback would not think of throwing in his direction. For this reason, ironically, the best cornerbacks sometimes go completely unnoticed in a game. The longer a cornerback can stick to his receiver, the more time his teammates have to sack the quarterback. By shutting down the passing game this way, a cornerback lives for the interception—and the glory of the long touchdown return.

Some fans think Ron Woodson is the finest all-

When a cornerback does his job as well as Darrell Green, an interception and a TD can be the reward.

around athlete in football. At six-feet and 197 pounds, when he is not intercepting or deflecting passes, he is returning punts an average of 10.5 yards or kickoffs an average 21.8 yards—both Top-10 stats. Voted his team's MVP in 1990, Woodson has a Hall of Fame future in front of him. Who knows what might happen if he gets his wish to play both cornerback and wide receiver!

Cornerback Darrell Green won the 1990 "NFL Fastest Man" competition—for the second time. Judging from his interception and passes-deflected numbers, he also has hands like a pickpocket. Considered the key player in the Washington defense, Green is one of those deep backs who always draws the opposing team's top receiver.

What Woodson and Green have in steadiness and consistency, "Neon" Deion Sanders replaces with flash. An electrifying player whose other nicknames include "Prime Time" and "Money," Sanders led the 1990 Atlanta Falcons with 1,254 total yards. A feared breakaway artist on kickoff and punt returns, he also ran back a couple of interceptions for 61- and 82-yard TDs. Cornerback might yet be the most exciting position in defensive football.

When a fan turns to the record books in search of lifetime interception leaders, a couple of Hall of Fame cornerbacks hold down the number two and three positions. They are Emlen Tunnell of the Giants (with 79) and Dick "Night Train" Lane of the Lions (68). Both had their greatest years in the 1950s. They are legends of the game who set high standards of excellence for cornerbacks once and for all.

Safeties

It used to be that cornerbacks got all the glory, and safeties just helped out. They were insurance. They were the last-chance tacklers who would be seen diving for the heels of a wide receiver who outran his cornerback down the field for a touchdown.

Today, all that has changed. Safeties are now more like linebackers with cornerback speed, and are among the most feared defenders. No longer do they just play the run and cover the middle. They must be able to outrun the fastest wide receiver. They must also be tall and flexible enough to outwit and outmaneuver the pass-catchers. They need a middle linebacker's quick reflexes and the brains to read each situation. Finally, they must be tough enough to own the middle, to take it away from the offense's passing game, and to dare receivers to come in and look for an easy reception. The 1980s brought this kind of safety to pro football.

*Even a hard-working safety such as Joey Browner is grateful for
a break while his offense takes the field.*

*Mark Carrier (20) earned the NFL's Defensive Rookie of the Year
in 1990 for interceptions like this one.*

It is hard to say which safety is today's best, but if
a vote were taken Vikings' Pro Bowl veteran Joey
Browner would be right up at the top. Known as the
nastiest and the craftiest, in 1989 Browner was second
on his team with 112 tackles. A year later, he recorded a
personal high of seven interceptions and 120 tackles!

These kinds of statistics prove that the safety no
longer roams around in the secondary waiting for
somebody else to do the job. Also, safeties today are
developing reputations as "hit masters" for their
spectacular tackles. And no one is as fierce as Ronnie
Lott. Lott is an eight-time Pro Bowler who anchored the
powerhouse, Super Bowl-winning 49er teams of the
1980s. During that decade, Lott set the standard by

Highest Career Interceptions

	Years	No.	Yards	TD
Paul Krause	16	81	1,185	3
Emlen Tunnell	14	79	1,282	4
Dick "Night Train" Lane	14	68	1,207	5
Ken Riley	15	65	596	5
Dick Le Beau	13	62	762	3
Dave Brown	15	62	698	5

which all future safeties must measure themselves.

Tim McDonald of the Phoenix Cardinals is a young safety many think of as the new Ronnie Lott. In the 1990 season, McDonald led the Cards in tackles with 132—101 of them unassisted. He also racked up four interceptions and a pair of forced fumbles. Once the rest of his team picks up on his winning ways, he is sure to attain the superstar status he deserves.

As the 1990 NFL Defensive Rookie of the Year, Mark Carrier is proof that safeties might rule for another ten years. In his first professional season, Carrier led all comers with a team-record ten interceptions and made the Pro Bowl. He demonstrated his intensity and superb instincts during a game against the Redskins when he picked off three passes.

Without a doubt, fans looking for the play's finest action should direct their eyes to the secondary, where safeties are revolutionizing the game. Currently, only one safety—Willie Wood—has entered the Hall of Fame (class of 1989). This will change. Today, a great safety is a helmet-splitting tackler who is in on most every play. A truly great safety can control the game.

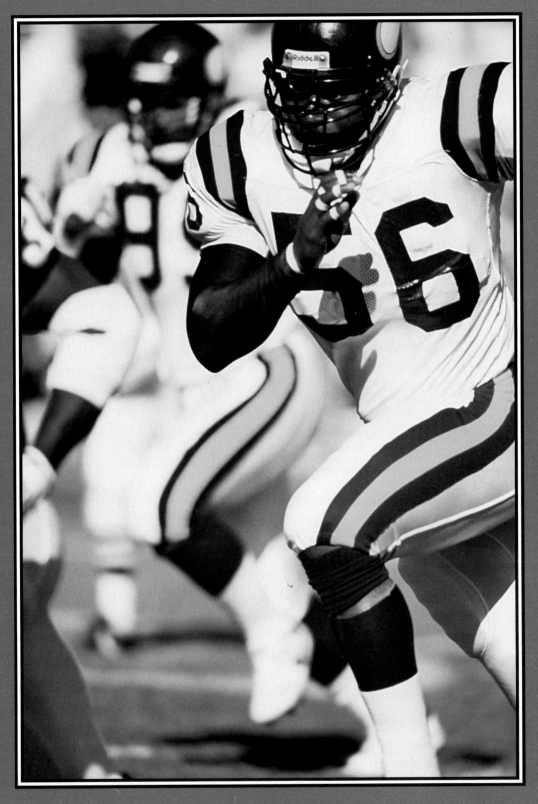

*Playing on special teams takes a fearless player like Chris Doleman of
the Minnesota Vikings.*

Special Teams

Coach Walt Michaels once said of special teams: "Everyone has some fear. A man who has no fear belongs in a mental institution. Or on special teams." On the same subject, Coach Dick Vermeil said, "If you have enthusiastic special teams, you have good special teams—no matter how they block, tackle, or run."

What are these guys talking about? Well, imagine that you are on a special team that defends the kickoff. Lined up across the field with your mates, the instant the ball is kicked you charge downfield after the receiver, without concern for life or limb. Teamwork is still important, but this is largely a job for war-whooping crazies who love to hit and be hit.

This does not mean that the special team game is without strategy. Good special teams help forge playoff contenders. It is no coincidence that the 1990 Super Bowl champion Giants had superb special teams.

Defense Trivia

Q: *Name the only defensive player to win the NFC Rookie of the Year award since 1980.*

A: *Mark Carrier, Chicago Bears safety, 1990.*

Q: *Name the three defensive players who have won the AFC Rookie of the Year award since 1980.*

A: *Leslie O'Neal, end (1986); Shane Conlan, linebacker (1987); Derrick Thomas, linebacker (1989).*

A blocker's worst nightmare: Howie Long in your face.

Their winning ways depended largely on controlling field position.

With the kickoff special team, the ball is teed on the 35-yard line and the kicker drops back about ten yards. The ten members of the special team fan out on either side of the kicker, five to a side. The players with the best pursuit skills are positioned closest to the ball. Those with the most speed are setup on the outside. The defenders close to the middle of the field charge headlong, looking to meet head-on and break up the wedge of blockers who group around the runner. The fleet-footed outside defenders hope to nail the runner after the blockers have been taken out.

Other special team situations are field goals, extra points, and punts. The players sent in to defend against these kicks are tall defensive linemen and linebackers with a talent for pass-rushing. Those set in the middle try to slice through for a direct block, or leap high in the air to swat down a long field goal. Successful blocks, however, are usually made by defenders with good speed who setup outside in an attempt to strike from an angle. On long field goal tries, two or three defenders are held back like safeties to try to thwart trick plays such as a fake kick. On particularly long field goal attempts, defenders might have to return kicks that fall short of the goal line.

Most of these defensive players are also used in punt coverage. This is a strange defensive setup in that linebackers, defensive ends, cornerbacks, and safeties are brought in to assume offensive positions to shield the punter. This works both ways: the special defensive team trying to block the punt will suddenly take on offensive blocking duties.

Three blockers, two upbacks, and a fullback take their stances in the backfield to protect the kicker. On the scrimmage line, the cornerbacks and safeties play

The quarterback is the target of defense.

wide toward the sidelines, as if they were ends hoping to race downfield in time to tackle the receiver. The linebackers, taking up what would normally be guard and tackle positions, block and hang tight until the ball is kicked. Then they move downfield to contain the play.

However important special teams are to all-around team defensive play, individuals are seldom recognized as heroes. Kickers and return artists get the glory. Special teams play strictly as a team. Scouting reports often speak of good or bad "coverage" without singling out this or that player for praise. Without tough-nosed special teams, however, a team with an otherwise dependable defense might play in vain. Imagine the frustration that must come when a strong defense shuts down the pass and run, only to have the special team let a punt receiver run the ball for a 60-yard touchdown!

How important is the defense? As any NFL coach will tell you, a team that hopes to win the Super Bowl can't do it without a great defensive team.

It's just another day at the office for Cornelius Bennett.

The Defensive Hall Of Fame

These players are all enshrined in the Pro Football Hall of Fame in Canton, Ohio. To be eligible, a player must be retired five years (coaches must only be retired). Players are listed with their year of induction.

Linemen

(played prior to World War II)

Turk Edwards	1969
Dan Fortmann	1985
Ed Healey	1964
Mel Hein	1963
Pete Henry	1963
Cal Hubbard	1963
Walt Kiesling	1966
Bruiser Kinard	1971
Link Lyman	1964
Mike Michalske	1964
George Musso	1982
Joe Stydahar	1967
George Trafton	1964
Bulldog Turner	1966
Alex Wojciechowicz	1968

Defensive Linemen

(modern NFL)

Doug Atkins	1982
Buck Buchanan	1990
Willie Davis	1981
Art Donovan	1968
Len Ford	1976
"Mean" Joe Greene	1987
Deacon Jones	1980
Bob Lilly	1980
Gino Marchetti	1972
Leo Nomellini	1969
Merlin Olsen	1982

Alan Page	1988
Andy Robustelli	1971
Ernie Stautner	1969
Arnie Weinmeister	1984
Bill Willis	1977

Linebackers

Bobby Bell	1983
Dick Butkus	1979
George Connor	1975
Bill George	1974
Jack Ham	1988
Ted Hendricks	1990
Sam Huff	1982
Jack Lambert	1990
Willie Lanier	1986
Ray Nitschke	1978
Joe Schmidt	1973

Defensive Backs

Herb Adderley	1980
Mel Blount	1989
Willie Brown	1984
Jack Christiansen	1970
Ken Houston	1986
Dick "Night Train" Lane	1974
Yale Lary	1979
Emlen Tunnell	1967
Larry Wilson	1978
Willie Wood	1989

Stats

Super MVPs

The following defensive players were named Most Valuable Player in a Super Bowl.

Super Bowl	Player	Position	Team
V	Chuck Howley	Linebacker	Dallas
VII	Jake Scott	Safety	Miami
XII	Harvey Martin	End	Dallas
XII	Randy White	Tackle	Dallas
XX	Richard Dent	End	Chicago

Highest Kickoff Return Average †

	Years	No.	Yards	Avg.	TD
Gale Sayers	7	91	2,781	30.6	6
Lynn Chandnois	7	92	2,720	29.6	3
Abe Woodson	9	193	5,538	28.7	5
Buddy Young	6	90	2,514	27.9	2
Travis Williams	5	102	2,801	27.5	6

† Minimum 75 Returns

Safeties

	Years	No.
Ted Hendricks	15	4
Doug English	10	4

Glossary

BLINDSIDE. To tackle the quarterback from behind as he is setting up to pass.

BLITZ. A fierce pass rush in which linebackers and deep backs charge the quarterback.

COVERAGE. Defense against the pass.

DIME DEFENSE. Six pass defenders in the backfield.

DOG. A fierce pass rush by one or more linebackers.

FAIR CATCH. A punt or kickoff reception free of tacklers. A player raises one arm in the air to signal a fair catch. He cannot run the football, and he cannot be touched. Penalties are given if either of these things happen.

FLEX. Seven defensive players near the line of scrimmage.

KEY. A movement or setup on the offensive team that clues a defender about blocking patterns and the possible direction of play.

MAN-TO-MAN. Pass coverage where one defender covers one eligible receiver.

NICKEL DEFENSE. Five pass defenders in the backfield.

PASS PATTERN. The path or route a receiver moves through to get open and catch the ball.

PENETRATION. The degree of success that the defensive front line has crossing the scrimmage line.

SCRIMMAGE LINE. The line where the play begins, running through the center of the ball from sideline to sideline.

SECONDARY. The backfield.

SLANT. When a defensive lineman charges to the left or right of his opponent rather than head-on.

STACK. When a linebacker lines up directly behind a defensive lineman.

STRONGSIDE. That side of the offensive line where the tight end takes position.

STUNT. Where two defensive players switch rushing paths just after the ball is snapped.

WEAKSIDE. That side of the offensive line without the tight end.

ZONE DEFENSE. Defending a specific area in the backfield.

Picture Credits

Bibliography

Books

Barron, Bill, Larry Eldridge, Jr., Chuck Garrity, Jr.,Jim Natal, and Beau Riffenburgh. *The Illustrated NFL Playbook*. New York: Workman Publishing, 1988.

Butkus, Dick. *Inside Defensive Football*. Chicago: Henry Regnery Company, 1972.

Carroll, Bob, Pete Palmer, and John Thorn. *The Hidden Game of Football*. New York: Warner Books, 1988.

Cohen, Richard M., and David S. Neft. *The Sports Encyclopedia: Pro Football*. New York: St. Martin's Press, 1991.

Hollander, Zander, ed. *The Complete Handbook of Pro Football*. New York: Signet, 1991.

Lamb, Kevin. *Quarterbacks, Nickelbacks, and Other Loose Change*. Chicago: Contemporary Books, 1984.

Periodicals

Lamb, Kevin, and Chris Mortensen. "The NFL's Best." *Sport*, October 1991: 40.

Meisel, Barry. "Sack Masters." *Sport*, August 1991: 74.

Meisel, Barry. "Today's Strong Safeties Really Are Strong (and Fast and Tough and Mean)..." *Sport*, August 1991: 50.

Miller, J. David. "The NFL's Super 78." *Sport*, August 1990: 37.

Miller, J. David. "Heavy Hitters from Hell." *Sport*, August 1991: 32.

Zimmerman, Paul. "Out of the Running." *Sports Illustrated*, October 8, 1990: 52.

Index

DATE DUE

GAYLORD			PRINTED IN U.S.A.